My Daily Affirmations

I AM COURAGEOUS

Mood: ☹ ☹ 😐 ☺ 😃   Date:

I feel good about myself because...

Today, I forgive myself for...

Reflection   Reminder

_____   _____

_____   _____

_____   _____

_____   _____

DAILY SELF LOVE NOTE

I AM ENOUGH

Mood: ☹ ☹ 😐 ☺ 😄   Date:

I feel good about myself because...

Today, I forgive myself for...

Reflection   Reminder

_____   _____

_____   _____

_____   _____

_____   _____

DAILY SELF LOVE NOTE

I AM STRONG

Mood: ☹ ☹ 😐 ☺ 😃   Date:

I feel good about myself because...

Today, I forgive myself for...

Reflection   Reminder

_____   _____

_____   _____

_____   _____

_____   _____

DAILY SELF LOVE NOTE

I AM IMPORTANT

Mood: ☹ ☹ 😐 ☺ 😀   Date:

I feel good about myself because...

Today, I forgive myself for...

Reflection   Reminder

_____   _____

_____   _____

_____   _____

_____   _____

DAILY SELF LOVE NOTE

I AM EXTRODINARY

Mood: ☹ ☹ 😐 ☺ 😃   Date:

I feel good about myself because...

Today, I forgive myself for...

Reflection   Reminder

_____   _____

_____   _____

_____   _____

_____   _____

DAILY SELF LOVE NOTE

I AM AN AMAZING PERSON

Mood: ☹ ☹ 😐 🙂 😄   Date:

I feel good about myself because...

Today, I forgive myself for...

Reflection   Reminder

_____   _____

_____   _____

_____   _____

_____   _____

DAILY SELF LOVE NOTE

I AM A LEADER

Mood: 😧 ☹️ 😐 🙂 😃   Date:

I feel good about myself because...

Today, I forgive myself for...

Reflection   Reminder

_____   _____

_____   _____

_____   _____

_____   _____

DAILY SELF LOVE NOTE

THERE IS NO ONE BETTER THAN YOU

Mood: ☹ ☹ 😐 🙂 😄   Date:

I feel good about myself because...

Today, I forgive myself for...

Reflection   Reminder

_____   _____

_____   _____

_____   _____

_____   _____

DAILY SELF LOVE NOTE

I CHOOSE MY ATTITUDE

Mood: ☹ ☹ 😐 ☺ 😃   Date:

I feel good about myself because...

Today, I forgive myself for...

Reflection   Reminder

_____   _____

_____   _____

_____   _____

_____   _____

DAILY SELF LOVE NOTE

I ALWAYS MATTER

Mood: ☹ ☹ 😐 ☺ 😃   Date:

I feel good about myself because...

Today, I forgive myself for...

Reflection   Reminder

_____   _____

_____   _____

_____   _____

_____   _____

DAILY SELF LOVE NOTE

I CAN GET THROUGH ANYTHING

Mood: ☹ ☹ 😐 ☺ 😃   Date:

I feel good about myself because...

Today, I forgive myself for...

Reflection   Reminder

_____   _____

_____   _____

_____   _____

_____   _____

DAILY SELF LOVE NOTE

I AM CAPABLE OF ANYTHING

Mood: ☹ ☹ 😐 ☺ 😀   Date:

I feel good about myself because...

Today, I forgive myself for...

Reflection   Reminder

_____   _____

_____   _____

_____   _____

_____   _____

DAILY SELF LOVE NOTE

I CONTROL MY OWN HAPPINESS

Mood: ☹ ☹ 😐 ☺ 😄   Date:

I feel good about myself because...

Today, I forgive myself for...

Reflection   Reminder

_____   _____

_____   _____

_____   _____

_____   _____

DAILY SELF LOVE NOTE

I DON'T GIVE UP

Mood: ☹ ☹ 😐 ☺ 😃   Date:

I feel good about myself because...

Today, I forgive myself for...

Reflection   Reminder

_____   _____

_____   _____

_____   _____

_____   _____

DAILY SELF LOVE NOTE

I AM SPECIAL

Mood: ☹ ☹ 😐 ☺ 😃   Date:

I feel good about myself because...

Today, I forgive myself for...

Reflection   Reminder

_____   _____

_____   _____

_____   _____

_____   _____

DAILY SELF LOVE NOTE

I LOVE ME

Mood: ☹ ☹ 😐 ☺ 😄   Date:

I feel good about myself because...

Today, I forgive myself for...

Reflection   Reminder

_____   _____

_____   _____

_____   _____

_____   _____

DAILY SELF LOVE NOTE

I AM GRATEFUL FOR WHO I AM

Mood: ☹ ☹ 😐 ☺ 😄   Date:

I feel good about myself because...

Today, I forgive myself for...

Reflection   Reminder

_____   _____

_____   _____

_____   _____

_____   _____

DAILY SELF LOVE NOTE

I PUT MYSELF FIRST

Mood: ☹ ☹ 😐 ☺ 😀   Date:

I feel good about myself because...

Today, I forgive myself for...

Reflection   Reminder

_____   _____

_____   _____

_____   _____

_____   _____

DAILY SELF LOVE NOTE

I USE MY GIFTS WITH LOVE, GRATITUDE AND PRIDE

Mood: ☹ ☹ 😐 ☺ 😃   Date:

I feel good about myself because...

Today, I forgive myself for...

Reflection   Reminder

_____   _____

_____   _____

_____   _____

_____   _____

DAILY SELF LOVE NOTE

I AM NOT AFRAID TO FAIL

Mood: ☹ ☹ 😐 🙂 😃   Date:

I feel good about myself because...

Today, I forgive myself for...

Reflection   Reminder

_____   _____

_____   _____

_____   _____

_____   _____

DAILY SELF LOVE NOTE

I HAVE INNER PEACE

Mood: ☹ ☹ 😐 ☺ 😄   Date:

I feel good about myself because...

Today, I forgive myself for...

Reflection   Reminder

_____   _____

_____   _____

_____   _____

_____   _____

DAILY SELF LOVE NOTE

I HAVE EVERYTHING I NEED WITHIN MYSELF

Mood: ☹ ☹ 😐 ☺ 😃   Date:

I feel good about myself because...

Today, I forgive myself for...

Reflection

Reminder

_____   _____

_____   _____

_____   _____

_____   _____

DAILY SELF LOVE NOTE

I TRUST MY INSTINCTS

Mood: ☹ ☹ 😐 🙂 😄   Date:

I feel good about myself because...

Today, I forgive myself for...

Reflection   Reminder

_____   _____

_____   _____

_____   _____

_____   _____

DAILY SELF LOVE NOTE

I HAVE A KIND HEART

Mood: ☹ ☹ 😐 ☺ 😃   Date:

I feel good about myself because...

Today, I forgive myself for...

Reflection

Reminder

_____   _____

_____   _____

_____   _____

_____   _____

DAILY SELF LOVE NOTE

ALL MY WORDS HAVE POWER

Mood: ☹ ☹ 😐 ☺ 😃   Date:

I feel good about myself because...

Today, I forgive myself for...

Reflection   *Reminder*

_____   _____

_____   _____

_____   _____

_____   _____

DAILY SELF LOVE NOTE

I CAN BE ANYTHING I WANT TO BE

Mood: ☹ ☹ 😐 ☺ 😃   Date:

I feel good about myself because...

Today, I forgive myself for...

Reflection   Reminder

_____   _____

_____   _____

_____   _____

_____   _____

DAILY SELF LOVE NOTE

I HAVE RESPECT FOR OTHERS

Mood: ☹ ☹ 😐 ☺ 😄   Date:

I feel good about myself because...

Today, I forgive myself for...

Reflection   Reminder

_____   _____

_____   _____

_____   _____

_____   _____

DAILY SELF LOVE NOTE

MY PARENTS ARE PROUD OF ME

Mood: ☹ ☹ 😐 ☺ 😃   Date:

I feel good about myself because...

Today, I forgive myself for...

Reflection   *Reminder*

_____   _____

_____   _____

_____   _____

_____   _____

DAILY SELF LOVE NOTE

I HAVE BIG DREAMS

Mood: ☹ ☹ 😐 ☺ 😃   Date:

I feel good about myself because...

Today, I forgive myself for...

Reflection   Reminder

_____   _____

_____   _____

_____   _____

_____   _____

DAILY SELF LOVE NOTE

I AM PROUD OF WHO I AM

Mood: ☹ ☹ 😐 🙂 😃   Date:

I feel good about myself because...

Today, I forgive myself for...

Reflection   Reminder

_____   _____

_____   _____

_____   _____

_____   _____

DAILY SELF LOVE NOTE

I AM POSITIVE

Mood: ☹ ☹ ☺ ☺ ☺   Date:

I feel good about myself because...

Today, I forgive myself for...

Reflection   Reminder

_____   _____

_____   _____

_____   _____

_____   _____

DAILY SELF LOVE NOTE

I WILL NOT COMPARE MYSELF TO OTHERS

Mood: ☹ ☹ 😐 ☺ 😃   Date:

I feel good about myself because...

Today, I forgive myself for...

Reflection   *Reminder*

_____   _____

_____   _____

_____   _____

_____   _____

DAILY SELF LOVE NOTE

I AM HAPPY FOR THE SUCCESS OF OTHERS

Mood: ☹ ☹ 😐 ☺ 😃   Date:

I feel good about myself because...

Today, I forgive myself for...

Reflection   Reminder

_____   _____

_____   _____

_____   _____

_____   _____

DAILY SELF LOVE NOTE

I AM TRUSTWORTHY

Mood: ☹ 😟 😐 🙂 😄   Date:

I feel good about myself because...

Today, I forgive myself for...

Reflection   Reminder

_____   _____

_____   _____

_____   _____

_____   _____

DAILY SELF LOVE NOTE

I HAVE MANY GIFTS AND TALENTS

Mood: ☹ ☹ 😐 ☺ 😀   Date:

I feel good about myself because...

Today, I forgive myself for...

Reflection   Reminder

_____   _____

_____   _____

_____   _____

_____   _____

DAILY SELF LOVE NOTE

I CAN BE ANYTHING I WANT TO BE

Mood: ☹ ☹ 😐 ☺ 😄   Date:

I feel good about myself because...

Today, I forgive myself for...

Reflection   Reminder

_____   _____

_____   _____

_____   _____

_____   _____

DAILY SELF LOVE NOTE

I AM PATIENT

Mood: ☹ ☹ 😐 ☺ 😃   Date:

I feel good about myself because...

Today, I forgive myself for...

Reflection   Reminder

_____   _____

_____   _____

_____   _____

_____   _____

DAILY SELF LOVE NOTE

I HAVE THE POWER TO MAKE MY DREAMS COME TRUE

Mood: ☹ ☹ 😐 ☺ 😃   Date:

I feel good about myself because...

Today, I forgive myself for...

Reflection   Reminder

_____   _____

_____   _____

_____   _____

_____   _____

DAILY SELF LOVE NOTE

I FIND WAYS TO SMILE OFTEN

Mood: ☹ ☹ ☺ ☺ 😀   Date:

I feel good about myself because...

Today, I forgive myself for...

Reflection   Reminder

_____   _____

_____   _____

_____   _____

_____   _____

DAILY SELF LOVE NOTE

I AM BOLD

Mood: 😠 😟 😐 🙂 😀   Date:

I feel good about myself because...

Today, I forgive myself for...

Reflection   Reminder

_____   _____

_____   _____

_____   _____

_____   _____

DAILY SELF LOVE NOTE

I AM CARING

Mood: ☹ ☹ 😐 🙂 😃   Date:

I feel good about myself because...

Today, I forgive myself for...

Reflection   Reminder

_____   _____

_____   _____

_____   _____

_____   _____

DAILY SELF LOVE NOTE

I LOVE LEARNING

Mood: ☹ ☹ 😐 ☺ 😃   Date:

I feel good about myself because...

Today, I forgive myself for...

Reflection   Reminder

_____   _____

_____   _____

_____   _____

_____   _____

DAILY SELF LOVE NOTE

MY LIFE IS WONDERFUL

Mood: ☹ ☹ 😐 ☺ 😄   Date:

I feel good about myself because...

Today, I forgive myself for...

Reflection   Reminder

_____   _____

_____   _____

_____   _____

_____   _____

DAILY SELF LOVE NOTE

I AM WISE

Mood: ☹ ☹ 😐 ☺ 😀   Date:

I feel good about myself because...

Today, I forgive myself for...

Reflection   Reminder

_____   _____

_____   _____

_____   _____

_____   _____

DAILY SELF LOVE NOTE

I AM A PROBLEM SOLVER

Mood: ☹ ☹ 😐 🙂 😃   Date:

I feel good about myself because...

Today, I forgive myself for...

Reflection   Reminder

_____   _____

_____   _____

_____   _____

_____   _____

DAILY SELF LOVE NOTE

I AM FUNNY

Mood: ☹ ☹ 😐 ☺ 😃   Date:

I feel good about myself because...

Today, I forgive myself for...

Reflection   Reminder

_____   _____

_____   _____

_____   _____

_____   _____

DAILY SELF LOVE NOTE

I AM A GREAT FRIEND

Mood: ☹ ☹ 😐 ☺ 😄   Date:

I feel good about myself because...

Today, I forgive myself for...

Reflection   Reminder

_____   _____

_____   _____

_____   _____

_____   _____

DAILY SELF LOVE NOTE

I AM ADVENTUROUS

Mood: ☹ ☹ 😐 ☺ 😄   Date:

I feel good about myself because...

Today, I forgive myself for...

Reflection   Reminder

_____   _____

_____   _____

_____   _____

_____   _____

DAILY SELF LOVE NOTE

I HAVE A STRONG BODY

Mood: ☹ ☹ 😐 ☺ 😀   Date:

I feel good about myself because...

Today, I forgive myself for...

Reflection   Reminder

_____   _____

_____   _____

_____   _____

_____   _____

DAILY SELF LOVE NOTE

NEVER FORGET
YOU ARE ALWAYS
ENOUGH, NEVER
LET ANYONE
CHANGE WHO YOU
ARE!

Made in the USA
Coppell, TX
08 February 2023

12424556R00057